Neanderthals

H.-G. Saenger

The Book:

The Enduring Legacy of Neanderthals

In this book, we have explored the fascinating world of Neanderthals, delving into their evolutionary history, anatomy, culture, technology, and interactions with modern humans. As we continue to uncover more about our ancient relatives, it is crucial to remember the importance of studying Neanderthals.

The Author:

H.-G. Saenger

Passionate reader

and versatile author.

Lives since 2020 with his second wife

wife in Thailand

Neanderthals

Unraveling the Secrets of Our Ancient Relatives

by

H.-G. Saenger

Table of Contents

Tools and Technology: The Neanderthal Innovators

- Stone tool technology: The Mousterian industry
- Innovation and problem-solving skills
- Neanderthal hunting strategies and weapons

The Neanderthal Diet: What Our Ancestors Ate

- Dietary staples and food sources
- Cooking and food processing techniques
- The impact of diet on Neanderthal health

Neanderthal-Modern Human Interactions: Encounters and Interbreeding

- The first encounters between Neanderthals and modern humans
- Evidence of interbreeding and its implications
- Genetic legacy: Neanderthal DNA in modern humans

The Mysterious Disappearance: Extinction of the Neanderthals

- Theories explaining the Neanderthal extinction
- Environmental factors and climate change
- Competition and possible conflicts with modern humans

Unearthing the Past: Neanderthal Fossils and Archaeological Discoveries

- Notable Neanderthal fossil finds
- The role of archaeology in understanding Neanderthal life

- Modern techniques for analyzing Neanderthal remains

Advancements in Neanderthal Research: Decoding the Neanderthal Genome

- The Neanderthal genome project
- Insights gained from genetic research
- Ethical considerations in Neanderthal research

The Enduring Legacy of Neanderthals

In this book, we have explored the fascinating world of Neanderthals, delving into their evolutionary history, anatomy, culture, technology, and interactions with modern humans. As we continue to uncover more about our ancient relatives, it is crucial to remember the importance of studying Neanderthals. Not only do they provide invaluable insights into our own evolutionary history, but they also serve as a reminder of the incredible adaptability and resilience of the human species. By understanding the lives of Neanderthals, we can better comprehend our place in the world and our shared human story.

Introduction: The Fascinating World of Neanderthals

The Importance of Studying Neanderthals

Studying Neanderthals is an essential part of understanding our own evolutionary history and human development. As our closest extinct relatives, Neanderthals can provide us with unique insights into various aspects of human evolution, culture, and biology. There are several reasons why studying Neanderthals is so important:

Understanding Human Evolution: By examining Neanderthals, we can learn more about the evolutionary process that led to the development of Homo sapiens. Studying the similarities and differences between Neanderthals and modern humans helps us understand the factors that influenced our own species' development and success.

Genetic Insights: Research into the Neanderthal genome has revealed that modern humans share a small percentage of Neanderthal DNA, a result of interbreeding between the two species. Understanding this genetic legacy can help us learn more about the impact of Neanderthal genes on modern human health, disease susceptibility, and even behavioral traits.

Cultural Development: By examining the social and cultural aspects of Neanderthal life, we can gain insights into the development of early human societies. Neanderthals had complex social structures, tool-making abilities, and possibly even art and symbolic expressions. Studying these aspects of their culture can help us understand the origins of our own social and cultural practices.

Adaptability and Resilience: Neanderthals were able to survive and thrive in harsh environments, such as the ice age landscapes of Europe and western Asia. By studying their anatomy, genetics, and technology, we can learn more about how they adapted to these challenging conditions and what factors may have contributed to their ultimate extinction.

Dispelling Myths and Stereotypes: Many misconceptions about Neanderthals persist, such as the belief that they were unintelligent or brutish. Studying Neanderthals helps us challenge these stereotypes and develop a more accurate and nuanced understanding of their lives and capabilities.

In conclusion, studying Neanderthals is vital for understanding our own evolutionary history, as well as the development of human culture and society. As we continue to unearth new discoveries about these fascinating relatives, we can deepen our understanding of what it means to be human and appreciate the complexities of our shared past.

Common Misconceptions about Neanderthals

Despite ongoing research and discoveries, several misconceptions about Neanderthals persist in popular culture. These misconceptions often perpetuate an inaccurate image of our ancient relatives. Here, we debunk some of the most common myths surrounding Neanderthals:

Neanderthals were stupid: One of the most widespread misconceptions is that Neanderthals were not as intelligent as modern humans. In reality, Neanderthals had a brain size comparable to ours, and there is evidence of their complex tool-making abilities, problem-solving skills, and potential use of symbolism in art and ritual. These findings suggest that Neanderthals possessed cognitive capacities similar to modern humans.

Neanderthals were brutish and violent: The stereotype of the Neanderthal as a savage, violent creature is another common myth. While it is true that Neanderthals led challenging lives and engaged in hunting, there is no evidence to suggest they were inherently more violent than other hominids of their time or even modern humans. Neanderthal burial sites and care for the injured or elderly individuals indicate a capacity for compassion and social cohesion.

Neanderthals were a primitive, inferior species: Some people mistakenly believe that Neanderthals were a less evolved, primitive version of modern humans. In fact, Neanderthals were a distinct species that evolved alongside Homo sapiens, with unique adaptations and characteristics. They were well-suited to their environment and had developed their own sophisticated culture and technology.

Neanderthals were strictly carnivorous: While it is true that Neanderthals relied heavily on meat in their diet, particularly in colder regions, they were not strictly carnivorous. Evidence suggests that they also consumed a variety of plant-based foods, such as nuts, fruits, and vegetables. Their diet was more varied and adaptable than previously thought.

Neanderthals and modern humans did not interact: Many people believe that Neanderthals and modern humans lived entirely separate lives. However, genetic research has revealed that these two species interbred, leaving traces of Neanderthal DNA in the genomes of modern humans. Moreover, archaeological evidence suggests that Neanderthals and modern humans may have lived in close proximity and possibly even exchanged ideas and technology.

By dispelling these misconceptions, we can develop a more accurate and nuanced understanding of Neanderthals and their place in human evolutionary history. Acknowledging the complexities of their lives, culture, and interactions with modern humans helps us appreciate the richness of our shared past and the connections that link us to these fascinating ancient relatives.

The Objective of This Book

The primary objective of this book is to provide readers with a comprehensive and engaging exploration of the world of Neanderthals. By delving into various aspects of Neanderthal life, culture, and evolutionary history, this book aims to:

Educate and Inform: Present accurate, up-to-date information about Neanderthals, drawing from the latest research and archaeological findings. By sharing this knowledge, the book aims to expand readers' understanding of these fascinating ancient relatives and their role in human history.

Dispel Myths and Stereotypes: Challenge common misconceptions about Neanderthals by presenting evidence-based information that paints a more accurate and nuanced picture of their lives, capabilities, and interactions with modern humans.

Highlight the Importance of Studying Neanderthals: Emphasize the significance of Neanderthal research in understanding our own evolutionary history, cultural development, and genetic heritage. By exploring the reasons for studying Neanderthals, this book seeks to encourage further research and foster a deeper appreciation for our shared past.

Provide a Comprehensive Overview: Offer a well-rounded exploration of Neanderthal life by covering various topics, including evolutionary history, anatomy, culture, technology, diet, interactions with modern humans, and the reasons for their extinction. This comprehensive approach allows readers to gain a holistic understanding of Neanderthals and their place in the larger narrative of human evolution.

Engage and Inspire: Present the information in a captivating, conversational style, making the content accessible and engaging for a broad audience. By making the world of Neanderthals come alive for readers, this book hopes to inspire curiosity and ignite a passion for learning more about our ancient relatives and the fascinating story of human evolution.

By achieving these objectives, this book aims to provide readers with a deeper understanding of Neanderthals, their importance in human history, and the ongoing relevance of studying these ancient relatives. Ultimately, this book seeks to contribute to a greater appreciation for the richness of our shared past and the connections that link us to our Neanderthal ancestors.

The Evolutionary Timeline: A Deep Dive into Human Prehistory

The Hominid Family Tree

The hominid family tree represents the complex evolutionary relationships among various human and human-like species over millions of years. Hominids, or members of the family Hominidae, include all species that are more closely related to humans than to other great apes such as chimpanzees, gorillas, and orangutans. The hominid family tree can be divided into two main groups: the subfamily Ponginae, which includes orangutans and their extinct relatives, and the subfamily Homininae, which encompasses humans, gorillas, and chimpanzees.

Within the Homininae subfamily, there are three main branches:

Gorillini (Gorillas): This tribe includes the modern gorilla species and their extinct relatives. Gorillas are the largest of the living primates and are native to the forests of central Africa.

Panini (Chimpanzees and Bonobos): This tribe consists of the common chimpanzee, the bonobo, and their extinct relatives. Chimpanzees and bonobos share more than 98% of their DNA with humans, making them our closest living relatives.

Hominini (Humans and Their Ancestors): This tribe includes modern humans (Homo sapiens) and all extinct species that are more closely related to us than to chimpanzees. The Hominini tribe can be further divided into two subtribes: the Australopithecina, which includes the famous „Lucy" fossil and other early human ancestors, and the Hominina, which encompasses the Homo genus and its extinct relatives.

The Homo genus, to which modern humans belong, has a rich and diverse history, with multiple species that have emerged and gone extinct over the past few million years. Some notable members of the Homo genus include:

Homo habilis: The earliest known species of the Homo genus, dating back to approximately 2.4 million years ago. Homo habilis is thought to be one of the first hominids to use stone tools.

Homo erectus: A more advanced hominid species that lived between 1.9 million and 140,000 years ago. Homo erectus is known for its upright posture, advanced tool use, and potential control of fire.

Homo neanderthalensis (Neanderthals): Our closest extinct relatives, Neanderthals lived in Europe and western Asia between approximately 400,000 and 40,000 years ago. They are known for their distinctive anatomy, advanced tool-making abilities, and potential cultural practices.

Homo sapiens (Modern Humans): The only surviving members of the Homo genus, modern humans first appeared around 300,000 years ago in Africa. Homo sapiens are characterized by their large brains, complex culture, and advanced technology.

The hominid family tree is a testament to the incredible diversity and adaptability of our ancestors. By studying these various species and their evolutionary relationships, we can gain valuable insights into the factors that have shaped human development and the unique qualities that define us as a species.

The Emergence of Neanderthals

Neanderthals, or Homo neanderthalensis, emerged as a distinct species within the Homo genus approximately 400,000 years ago. They are believed to have evolved from a common ancestor shared with modern humans (Homo sapiens), which likely lived around 500,000 to 700,000 years ago. The emergence of Neanderthals can be understood within the context of the broader hominid evolutionary timeline and the unique environmental factors that influenced their development.

Ancestral Origins: The exact ancestral species that gave rise to Neanderthals remains a subject of debate among scientists. However, it is widely accepted that Homo heidelbergensis, a species that lived in Africa and Europe between 700,000 and 200,000 years ago, may have been the common ancestor of both Neanderthals and modern humans. The populations of Homo heidelbergensis that migrated to Europe eventually evolved into Neanderthals, while those that remained in Africa evolved into Homo sapiens.

Adaptation to the European Environment: The emergence of Neanderthals was heavily influenced by the environmental conditions of Europe during the Pleistocene epoch, which was characterized by repeated glaciations and cold, harsh conditions. Neanderthals developed a range of adaptations that enabled them to survive in this challenging environment, including a stocky build to conserve heat, a large nasal cavity to warm and humidify the air, and a specialized metabolism to efficiently process a high-calorie, high-protein diet.

Genetic Divergence from Modern Humans: As Neanderthals and early Homo sapiens evolved separately in different geographic regions, they accumulated genetic differences that led to the distinct characteristics of each species. Recent advances in genetic research have allowed scientists to decode the Neanderthal genome and compare it to that of modern humans. This comparison has provided valuable insights into the unique traits of Neanderthals, as well as the genetic legacy they left behind through interbreeding with modern humans.

Cultural and Technological Development: In parallel with their anatomical and genetic evolution, Neanderthals also developed their own unique culture and technology. They are best known for their sophisticated stone tools, collectively referred to as the Mousterian industry. These tools, along with evidence of complex hunting strategies, social structures, and potential symbolic expressions, demonstrate the advanced cognitive abilities of Neanderthals and their capacity for innovation and adaptation.

In summary, the emergence of Neanderthals can be traced back to the divergence of European Homo heidelbergensis populations from their African counterparts. Over time, Neanderthals evolved a range of adaptations that allowed them to thrive in the challenging environments of Pleistocene Europe, while also developing their own distinct culture and technology. Understanding the emergence of Neanderthals is crucial for appreciating their role in human evolutionary history and the factors that contributed to their eventual extinction.

Neanderthals and Modern Humans: Common Ancestors and Divergent Paths

Neanderthals and modern humans share a complex evolutionary history that involves a common ancestry and subsequent divergence into distinct species. By examining the factors that led to their separate evolutionary paths and the unique characteristics of each species, we can gain a deeper understanding of human evolution as a whole.

Common Ancestors: It is widely accepted that Neanderthals and modern humans share a common ancestor, which is believed to be Homo heidelbergensis. This species lived in Africa and Europe between 700,000 and 200,000 years ago and displayed a mix of traits found in both Neanderthals and modern humans. As populations of Homo heidelbergensis migrated to different geographic regions, they became isolated from one another, setting the stage for the emergence of two distinct species.

Divergent Paths: The divergence of Neanderthals and modern humans can be traced back to approximately 500,000 to 700,000 years ago. The populations of Homo heidelbergensis that migrated to Europe eventually evolved into Neanderthals, while those that remained in Africa evolved into the ancestors of Homo sapiens. Over time, these separate populations developed unique genetic, anatomical, and cultural traits that defined their respective species.

Anatomical Differences: Neanderthals and modern humans display several key anatomical differences, many of which can be attributed to adaptations to their distinct environments. Neanderthals, adapted to the cold climates of Europe and western Asia, developed a stocky build, large nasal cavities, and a distinct brow ridge. In contrast, modern humans, who emerged in Africa, evolved a taller, more slender build, a flatter face, and a more rounded skull.

Cultural and Technological Divergence: As Neanderthals and modern humans evolved separately, they also developed their own unique cultures and technologies. Neanderthals are known for their sophisticated Mousterian stone tools and complex hunting strategies, while early Homo sapiens developed a more diverse range of technologies, including advanced projectile weapons and elaborate art and symbolic expressions. These cultural differences likely played a role in the success and expansion of modern humans, who eventually replaced Neanderthals and other hominid species.

Interbreeding and Genetic Legacy: Despite their separate evolutionary paths, there is evidence that Neanderthals and modern humans interacted and interbred. Genetic research has revealed that non-African modern human populations have inherited between 1-2% of their DNA from Neanderthals, a result of interbreeding that occurred when modern humans began migrating out of Africa. This genetic legacy has contributed to the unique traits and disease susceptibilities observed in present-day human populations.

In conclusion, the evolutionary history of Neanderthals and modern humans is characterized by a shared ancestry and subsequent divergence into distinct species. By examining the factors that drove their separate evolutionary paths and the unique traits of each species, we can gain valuable insights into the broader story of human evolution and the dynamic interplay between genetics, environment, and culture.

Neanderthal Anatomy: Distinct Features and Adaptations

Physical Characteristics of Neanderthals

Neanderthals (Homo neanderthalensis) were a distinct species of hominids that inhabited Europe and western Asia between 400,000 and 40,000 years ago. They displayed a unique set of physical characteristics that set them apart from modern humans (Homo sapiens) and allowed them to adapt to the challenging environments of the Pleistocene epoch. Some of the most notable physical characteristics of Neanderthals include:

Cranial Features: Neanderthals had a larger cranial capacity than modern humans, with an average brain size of 1,500 cubic centimeters. Their skulls were elongated and low, with a pronounced brow ridge and a receding forehead.

Facial Features: Neanderthals had a distinct facial morphology characterized by a projecting midface, a broad nose, and large nasal cavities. These features are thought to have helped warm and humidify cold, dry air, providing an advantage in the harsh climates of Pleistocene Europe.

Body Build: Neanderthals were shorter and stockier than modern humans, with a robust build and strong musculature. This body type is believed to have helped them conserve heat in the cold environments they inhabited. Males stood approximately 5'5" (165 cm) tall, while females were around 5'1" (155 cm).

Short Limbs: Neanderthals had relatively short limbs compared to modern humans, particularly in their lower legs and arms. This feature is another adaptation to cold climates, as shorter limbs reduce the surface area exposed to the cold and minimize heat loss.

Barrel-shaped Chest: Neanderthals had a wide, barrel-shaped chest, which provided ample space for their large lungs and heart. This feature may have contributed to their ability to cope with the physical demands of hunting large game and surviving in cold environments.

Dental Characteristics: Neanderthal teeth were larger and more robust than those of modern humans. They also displayed a unique feature called the „taurodont" pattern, in which the pulp cavity of the molars is enlarged, and the roots are short and fused. This dental morphology may have helped them process the tough, fibrous plant materials that were part of their diet.

Posture and Gait: Neanderthals had a slightly different posture and gait compared to modern humans, with a more forward-projecting center of mass and a wider pelvis. These features likely affected their locomotion, making them more adapted for power and stability rather than endurance and long-distance running.

These physical characteristics not only distinguish Neanderthals from modern humans but also reflect their unique adaptations to the challenging environments of Pleistocene Europe and western Asia.

Genetic Adaptations to Harsh Environments

Genetic adaptations play a critical role in the ability of a species to survive and thrive in harsh environments. Over time, through the process of natural selection, specific genetic traits that provide a survival advantage in a given environment become more prevalent within a population. Both modern humans and our ancient relatives, like the Neanderthals, developed genetic adaptations that allowed them to cope with the challenges of their respective environments.

Neanderthal Genetic Adaptations:

Neanderthals inhabited Europe and western Asia during the Pleistocene epoch, a time characterized by repeated glaciations and harsh climatic conditions. Some of the key genetic adaptations that enabled Neanderthals to survive in this challenging environment include:

Cold-Climate Adaptations: Neanderthals developed a number of genetic adaptations that helped them cope with the cold, such as increased body hair, a more efficient metabolism for generating heat, and a stocky build to minimize heat loss.

Metabolic Efficiency: Research suggests that Neanderthals possessed genetic adaptations that allowed them to efficiently process high-calorie, high-protein diets. This metabolic efficiency would have been essential for maintaining energy levels in the face of limited food resources.

Immune System Adaptations: Neanderthals likely faced a range of pathogens and disease risks in their environments. Genetic evidence indicates that they developed specific immune system adaptations that helped them combat these challenges, including genes related to the production of antimicrobial peptides and the regulation of immune responses.

Modern Human Genetic Adaptations:

Modern humans also developed genetic adaptations that allowed them to cope with a variety of challenging environments as they migrated across the globe. Some examples of these adaptations include:

High-Altitude Adaptations: Populations living at high altitudes, such as Tibetans, have genetic adaptations that enable them to cope with low oxygen levels. These adaptations include an increased production of hemoglobin and a more efficient use of oxygen by their cells.

Heat Adaptations: Populations living in hot, arid environments, such as the San people of southern Africa, have genetic adaptations that help them cope with high temperatures and water scarcity. These adaptations include genes related to increased sweating and the efficient regulation of body temperature.

Dietary Adaptations: As modern humans migrated to different regions, they encountered a wide range of food sources. This led to genetic adaptations related to diet, such as the ability to digest lactose in populations with a history of dairy farming or the development of amylase genes in populations with high-starch diets.

In summary, genetic adaptations have played a crucial role in the survival and success of both Neanderthals and modern humans in the face of diverse and challenging environments.

The Neanderthal Brain: Size and Cognitive Abilities

The Neanderthal brain has long been a subject of fascination and debate among scientists, as it provides valuable insights into the cognitive abilities of our closest extinct relatives. In this section, we will explore the size of the Neanderthal brain and what it can tell us about their cognitive capabilities.

Brain Size:

Neanderthals had a larger brain size compared to modern humans, with an average cranial capacity of approximately 1,500 cubic centimeters, while modern humans have an average capacity of around 1,350 cubic centimeters. This larger brain size has led some researchers to suggest that Neanderthals may have possessed comparable or even superior cognitive abilities to modern humans.

However, it is important to note that brain size alone is not a definitive indicator of intelligence or cognitive abilities. Other factors, such as the organization and connectivity of the brain, also play crucial roles in determining cognitive capabilities.

Cognitive Abilities:

While the exact cognitive abilities of Neanderthals remain a subject of ongoing research and debate, there is evidence to suggest that they possessed advanced cognitive skills. Some key indicators of Neanderthal cognitive abilities include:

Tool-Making: Neanderthals were skilled toolmakers, crafting sophisticated stone tools as part of the Mousterian industry. Their ability to produce these complex tools suggests advanced problem-solving skills, planning, and fine motor control.

Hunting Strategies: Neanderthals were successful hunters, capable of taking down large game such as mammoths and bison. The cooperative hunting strategies they employed required advanced communication, teamwork, and planning skills.

Social Structure: Evidence from Neanderthal burial sites and living arrangements suggests that they had complex social structures, with strong familial bonds and the potential for group cooperation. This implies a level of social cognition and empathy similar to that of modern humans.

Potential Symbolic Expression: While the evidence is still debated, some researchers argue that Neanderthals engaged in symbolic expression, such as the use of pigments or the creation of art. If true, this would indicate a capacity for abstract thought and self-awareness.

Interbreeding with Modern Humans: Genetic evidence shows that Neanderthals interbred with modern humans, which implies that they were capable of forming social bonds and engaging in complex interactions with another hominin species.

In conclusion, while the Neanderthal brain was larger than that of modern humans, brain size alone cannot provide a definitive measure of their cognitive abilities. The available evidence, however, suggests that Neanderthals possessed advanced cognitive skills, comparable in many ways to those of early modern humans.

Neanderthal Culture: Social Life, Art, and Rituals

Social Structure and Group Dynamics

Understanding the social structure and group dynamics of our ancient relatives, like the Neanderthals, can provide valuable insights into the evolution of human social behavior. While the exact nature of Neanderthal social structure remains a subject of debate, researchers have gathered evidence from various sources, including archaeological findings, to piece together a picture of their social organization.

Family Units and Small Groups:

Neanderthal social structure appears to have been based primarily on small family units or kin-based groups. Evidence from living sites and burials suggests that these family units were tightly knit, with members cooperating in activities such as hunting, food sharing, and raising offspring. The small group size likely allowed for a more intimate social environment, with close relationships between group members.

Cooperative Behavior:

Cooperative behavior was likely an essential aspect of Neanderthal social life, particularly in the context of hunting and resource sharing. The success of Neanderthal hunting strategies depended on the ability of group members to work together effectively. This suggests that Neanderthals had developed advanced communication skills and the capacity for teamwork and planning.

Hierarchy and Social Organization:

While the exact nature of the Neanderthal hierarchy and social organization is still unclear, some researchers speculate that their social structure was relatively egalitarian, with little evidence for centralized leadership or strict social hierarchies. This hypothesis is based on the lack of clear status indicators in the archaeological record, such as differential burial treatment or the presence of high-status artifacts.

Inter-group Relations:

The nature of inter-group relations among Neanderthals is not well understood, as evidence is scarce. However, some researchers suggest that Neanderthal groups maintained connections with other groups through trade, exchange of information, or inter-group mating. Genetic studies have also revealed that Neanderthals interbred with modern humans, suggesting that they were capable of forming social bonds and engaging in complex interactions with another hominin species.

Caring for the Injured and Elderly:

One notable aspect of Neanderthal social structure is the evidence for caring behavior toward the injured or elderly. Fossil remains have revealed individuals with significant injuries or disabilities that would have required assistance and care from others to survive. This suggests that Neanderthal groups displayed a level of empathy and compassion similar to that of modern humans.

In conclusion, while many aspects of Neanderthal social structure and group dynamics remain uncertain, the available evidence points to a social organization based on small family units with strong cooperative behavior and potentially egalitarian social relations.

Neanderthal Art and Symbolic Expressions

The question of whether Neanderthals engaged in art and symbolic expressions has long been a subject of debate among researchers. While early evidence was scarce, recent discoveries have shed new light on the potential artistic and symbolic behaviors of our closest extinct relatives. In this section, we will explore some of the key findings that suggest Neanderthals may have engaged in artistic and symbolic activities.

Use of Pigments: Several Neanderthal sites have revealed the presence of pigments, such as red ochre and manganese dioxide. These pigments may have been used for body decoration, tool coloring, or even creating art on cave walls. While the exact purpose of these pigments remains uncertain, their presence at multiple sites suggests that Neanderthals were interested in color and may have used it for symbolic purposes.

Engraved Patterns: In recent years, researchers have discovered engraved patterns on bones, stones, and cave walls at several Neanderthal sites. These patterns include lines, crosshatching, and geometric shapes. While the meaning and purpose of these engravings are still unclear, they suggest that Neanderthals were capable of creating abstract patterns, which could be considered a form of symbolic expression.

Possible Cave Art: In 2018, a study published in the journal Science presented evidence of cave art in Spain that predates the arrival of modern humans in the region by at least 20,000 years. This finding implies that the art was likely created by Neanderthals. If confirmed, this would represent the first known example of Neanderthal cave art and provide strong evidence for their capacity for symbolic expression.

Ornaments and Personal Adornment: While evidence for personal adornment among Neanderthals is limited, some discoveries suggest they may have used objects for decorative purposes. For example, eagle talons and shells with drilled holes have been found at Neanderthal sites, which could have been used as pendants or other forms of personal ornamentation.

Burial Practices: Neanderthal burial practices provide further evidence of their potential for symbolic expression. Some Neanderthal burials include grave goods, such as stone tools and animal bones, which could indicate a belief in an afterlife or the importance of these objects to the deceased individual. Additionally, some burials show signs of deliberate arrangement or the use of red ochre, suggesting that Neanderthals may have engaged in ritualistic or symbolic burial practices.

In summary, while the full extent of Neanderthal art and symbolic expressions remains a subject of ongoing research and debate, recent discoveries have provided intriguing evidence that suggests they may have engaged in artistic activities and possessed a capacity for abstract thought.

Burial Practices and the Concept of the Afterlife

Throughout human history, burial practices have often been linked to beliefs about the afterlife and the treatment of the deceased. Studying these practices can provide valuable insights into the spiritual and cultural aspects of ancient societies, including our extinct relatives, like the Neanderthals. In this section, we will explore the burial practices of Neanderthals and discuss what they might tell us about their concept of the afterlife.

Neanderthal Burial Practices:

Neanderthal burial practices have been a subject of debate among researchers for many years. While the number of confirmed Neanderthal burials is relatively small, some key aspects of their burial practices have emerged from the available evidence:

Intentional Burial: Some Neanderthal remains have been found in what appears to be deliberately dug graves, suggesting that they practiced intentional burial. This implies a level of care for the deceased and a possible belief in an afterlife or the importance of proper treatment of the dead.

Grave Goods: Several Neanderthal burials have been found with accompanying grave goods, such as stone tools, animal bones, or ornaments. The presence of these items could indicate that Neanderthals believed the deceased would need these objects in the afterlife, or they may have been included for symbolic or sentimental reasons.

Use of Pigments: Some Neanderthal burials show evidence of red ochre, a pigment that has been found at multiple Neanderthal sites. The use of red ochre in burials could have been symbolic, possibly representing blood or life force, or it may have had a ritualistic function.

Body Positioning: In some cases, Neanderthal remains have been found in specific body positions, such as a flexed or fetal position. This deliberate arrangement of the body could indicate a belief in the afterlife or a desire to provide comfort to the deceased.

Concept of the Afterlife:

While it is difficult to determine the exact beliefs of Neanderthals regarding the afterlife, their burial practices suggest that they may have held some concept of life after death or at least a spiritual connection to the deceased. The intentional burial of the dead, the inclusion of grave goods, and the use of pigments and body positioning all point to a level of care and attention that implies a belief in the significance of the deceased individual and their potential journey after death.

In conclusion, although the exact nature of Neanderthal beliefs about the afterlife remains uncertain, their burial practices provide evidence that they held a certain level of spiritual or symbolic understanding of death.

Tools and Technology: The Neanderthal Innovators

Stone Tool Technology: The Mousterian Industry

The Mousterian industry, named after the site of Le Moustier in France, is a stone tool technology that is strongly associated with Neanderthals. This technology, which emerged around 300,000 years ago and lasted until approximately 30,000 years ago, played a crucial role in the daily lives of Neanderthals and provides valuable insights into their cognitive abilities and cultural sophistication. In this section, we will explore the key features of the Mousterian industry and its significance for our understanding of Neanderthal technology.

Key Features of the Mousterian Industry:

Levallois Technique: The most distinctive aspect of the Mousterian industry is the use of the Levallois technique. This method involves the careful preparation of a stone core, followed by the removal of large, predetermined flakes, which could then be shaped into various tools. The Levallois technique allowed for greater control and predictability in the production of flakes, resulting in more efficient and standardized tools.

Variety of Tool Types: The Mousterian industry is characterized by a diverse range of tool types, including scrapers, points, and handaxes. This variety of tools suggests that Neanderthals had a complex understanding of the different functions and uses of these implements, allowing them to exploit a wide range of resources.

Specialization and Regional Variation: The Mousterian industry is known for its regional variations and specialization in certain tool types. For example, some sites show a higher concentration of specific tools, such as points or scrapers, which may reflect local adaptations to the environment or the availability of particular resources.

Retouching and Resharpening: Mousterian tools often show signs of retouching and resharpening, which indicates that Neanderthals maintained and modified their tools over time. This maintenance not only demonstrates their ability to plan for the future but also suggests that they had a deep understanding of the properties and limitations of their stone tools.

Significance of the Mousterian Industry for Understanding Neanderthal Technology:

The Mousterian industry provides important insights into the technological capabilities of Neanderthals. The complexity and sophistication of their stone tool technology, as demonstrated by the Levallois technique and the variety of tool types, indicate that Neanderthals possessed advanced cognitive abilities, including problem-solving skills, spatial reasoning, and fine motor control.

Additionally, the regional variation and specialization within the Mousterian industry suggest that Neanderthals were capable of adapting their tool-making strategies to suit the specific needs of their local environments. This adaptability and innovation further underscore the advanced technological capabilities of Neanderthals.

In conclusion, the Mousterian industry serves as a key example of Neanderthal stone tool technology, showcasing their advanced cognitive abilities, adaptability, and cultural sophistication.

Innovation and Problem-Solving Skills

Innovation and problem-solving skills are essential cognitive abilities that have played a crucial role in the evolution and survival of the human species. These skills allow us to create new solutions to challenges, adapt to changing environments, and develop new technologies. Neanderthals, as our closest extinct relatives, also demonstrated a remarkable capacity for innovation and problem-solving. In this section, we will explore some examples of Neanderthal innovation and problem-solving skills, which highlight their advanced cognitive abilities and cultural sophistication.

Stone Tool Technology: As previously discussed, the Mousterian industry is an excellent example of Neanderthal innovation and problem-solving skills. The development of the Levallois technique and the variety of tool types indicate that Neanderthals were capable of creating complex solutions to meet their various needs, such as hunting, food processing, and woodworking.

Adaptation to Harsh Environments: Neanderthals were able to survive and thrive in a wide range of environments, from the cold, glaciated landscapes of Europe to the more temperate regions of the Middle East. Their ability to adapt to these diverse environments demonstrates their capacity for innovation and problem-solving, as they developed new strategies for hunting, shelter, and clothing to suit the specific conditions of their surroundings.

Fire Use and Control: Neanderthals are known to have used and controlled fire, which was a significant technological innovation that required advanced problem-solving skills. Fire allowed them to cook food, stay warm in cold environments, and create better tools through the process of heat-treatment. The ability to use and control fire also suggests that Neanderthals had an understanding of cause-and-effect relationships and the ability to plan for the future.

Social Cooperation: The successful hunting strategies and group dynamics of Neanderthals required effective communication, coordination, and problem-solving skills. Cooperation among Neanderthal groups demonstrates their ability to work together to overcome challenges, such as the pursuit of large and dangerous prey or the sharing of limited resources.

Symbolic and Artistic Expression: As previously mentioned, there is growing evidence for Neanderthal art and symbolic expressions, such as the use of pigments, engraved patterns, and personal ornaments. These forms of expression imply that Neanderthals were capable of abstract thought and problem-solving on a symbolic level, which represents a significant cognitive achievement.

In conclusion, the innovation and problem-solving skills of Neanderthals are evident in various aspects of their technology, culture, and social organization. These cognitive abilities enabled them to adapt to diverse environments, develop advanced technologies, and create complex social structures.

Neanderthal Hunting Strategies and Weapons

Neanderthals were skilled hunters who relied heavily on a variety of hunting strategies and weapons to procure food and survive in their diverse environments. Understanding their hunting techniques and the tools they used can provide valuable insights into their cognitive abilities, social organization, and resourcefulness. In this section, we will explore Neanderthal hunting strategies and the weapons they employed to capture and process their prey.

Neanderthal Hunting Strategies:

Ambush Hunting: One of the primary hunting strategies employed by Neanderthals was ambush hunting, which involved hiding and waiting for prey to come within striking distance. This approach required patience, stealth, and an intimate knowledge of animal behavior and movement patterns.

Drive Hunting: Neanderthals also utilized drive hunting, a method that involves working together as a group to herd animals towards a specific location, such as a cliff or a narrow pass, where they could be more easily killed. This strategy required cooperation, communication, and coordination among group members.

Close-Range Hunting: Neanderthals are believed to have engaged in close-range hunting, using their strength and skill to confront large animals directly. This high-risk approach would have required a great deal of physical prowess, bravery, and tactical knowledge to be successful.

Neanderthal Weapons:

Spears: The most iconic weapon associated with Neanderthal hunting is the wooden spear, often tipped with a stone or bone point. These spears were likely used for thrusting or stabbing at close range, rather than being thrown. The production of these spears required a high level of skill in both woodworking and stone knapping.

Handaxes and Scrapers: Neanderthals also used handaxes and scrapers, which are common tools found within the Mousterian industry. Handaxes could have been used for a variety of purposes, including cutting meat, processing hides, and even as a weapon for hunting. Scrapers were primarily used for processing animal hides but could also have been used in hunting-related tasks.

Projectile Points: Some researchers have suggested that Neanderthals may have used projectile points, such as stone-tipped darts or throwing spears, for hunting at a distance. While evidence for this remains limited, the use of projectile weapons would demonstrate a more advanced level of hunting technology and strategy.

In conclusion, Neanderthal hunting strategies and weapons showcase their adaptability, resourcefulness, and advanced cognitive abilities. Their success as hunters was dependent on their intimate knowledge of their environment, their ability to work together as a group, and their skill in crafting a variety of specialized tools.

The Neanderthal Diet: What Our Ancestors Ate

Dietary Staples and Food Sources

Neanderthals lived in a diverse range of environments, and as a result, their diets were shaped by the availability of resources in their surroundings. By examining evidence from archaeological sites, stable isotope analysis, and dental wear patterns, researchers have been able to piece together a picture of the dietary staples and food sources that were important to Neanderthal survival. In this section, we will explore the key components of the Neanderthal diet and the various food sources that they relied upon.

Meat and Animal Protein:

Large Mammals: Neanderthals were primarily hunters, and their diet was heavily based on the consumption of large mammals. Some of the most common prey included species such as bison, horses, reindeer, and mammoths. These animals provided not only a rich source of protein but also fat, which was an essential energy source, particularly in colder environments.

Small Game: In addition to large mammals, Neanderthals also hunted smaller game, such as rabbits, birds, and rodents. These smaller animals would have provided a supplementary source of protein and diversified the Neanderthal diet.

Marine Resources: There is evidence that some Neanderthal populations living near coastal areas consumed marine resources, such as fish, shellfish, and marine mammals. These food sources would have provided additional sources of protein and essential nutrients, such as omega-3 fatty acids.

Plant-Based Foods:

Nuts and Seeds: Archaeological evidence suggests that Neanderthals consumed a variety of nuts and seeds, which provided important sources of fat, protein, and essential nutrients. Some of the nuts and seeds that have been found at Neanderthal sites include acorns, hazelnuts, and pine nuts.

Fruits and Berries: Neanderthals are also known to have consumed fruits and berries when they were in season. These plant-based foods provided a valuable source of carbohydrates, vitamins, and antioxidants.

Tubers and Roots: Some studies have found evidence that Neanderthals consumed tubers and roots, which would have been an important source of carbohydrates and dietary fiber. These plant-based foods would have helped to diversify their diet and provide additional energy sources.

Green Vegetables: There is also some evidence that Neanderthals consumed green vegetables, such as leafy plants and ferns. While these plant-based foods were likely a small part of their diet, they would have provided additional nutrients, such as vitamins and minerals.

In conclusion, the Neanderthal diet was primarily based on the consumption of meat from large mammals, supplemented by smaller game, marine resources, and a variety of plant-based foods. This diverse diet allowed them to survive and adapt to the different environments they inhabited, showcasing their resourcefulness and adaptability. By understanding the dietary staples and food sources of Neanderthals, we can gain valuable insights into their daily lives and the challenges they faced in their struggle for survival.

Cooking and Food Processing Techniques

Neanderthals not only relied on a diverse range of food sources but also employed various cooking and food processing techniques to make their meals more palatable, digestible, and nutritious. By examining archaeological evidence and the remains of food particles on Neanderthal tools, researchers have been able to deduce some of the methods they used to prepare their food. In this section, we will explore the cooking and food processing techniques employed by Neanderthals.

Cooking Techniques:

Fire: Neanderthals were known to use and control fire, which would have played a crucial role in their cooking techniques. Cooking food over an open fire would have not only made it more palatable but also increased its nutritional value by breaking down complex proteins and carbohydrates, making them easier to digest.

Roasting: One of the primary cooking methods used by Neanderthals was roasting, which involves cooking food directly over an open flame or on hot coals. Roasting meat and other foods would have helped to kill harmful bacteria, tenderize the meat, and enhance its flavor.

Boiling: Some researchers have suggested that Neanderthals may have used boiling as a cooking method, although direct evidence for this practice remains limited. Boiling food in water or other liquids would have allowed them to cook tougher cuts of meat, making them more tender and easier to eat.

Food Processing Techniques:

Butchering: Neanderthals were skilled at butchering large animals, which involved removing the skin, separating the meat from the bones, and processing the internal organs. Tools such as handaxes, knives, and scrapers would have been used to efficiently process the carcasses and obtain the maximum amount of usable meat.

Smashing Bones: Neanderthals are known to have smashed bones to extract the nutritious marrow inside, which was an important source of calories and fat. The use of specialized bone-crushing tools or simply smashing bones with rocks would have allowed them to access this valuable food source.

Grinding and Pounding: Some evidence suggests that Neanderthals used grinding and pounding techniques to process plant-based foods, such as nuts, seeds, and tubers. This would have involved the use of stones or other tools to crush and grind the food, making it easier to digest and releasing important nutrients.

Food Preservation: While there is limited direct evidence for food preservation techniques among Neanderthals, it is possible that they used methods such as drying, smoking, or fermenting to store and preserve their food for later consumption. These techniques would have allowed them to extend the shelf life of their food and ensure a more stable food supply.

In conclusion, Neanderthals employed various cooking and food processing techniques to make their meals more palatable, digestible, and nutritious. These methods demonstrate their advanced cognitive abilities and resourcefulness, as well as their understanding of the properties and limitations of their food sources.

The Impact of Diet on Neanderthal Health

The Neanderthal diet, which was primarily based on the consumption of meat from large mammals and supplemented by smaller game, marine resources, and a variety of plant-based foods, had a significant impact on their overall health and well-being. In this section, we will explore the ways in which the Neanderthal diet influenced their health, both positively and negatively.

Positive Impact on Health:

High Protein Intake: Neanderthals consumed a diet rich in animal protein, which would have provided essential amino acids needed for growth, tissue repair, and overall health. A high protein diet may have also contributed to their robust muscular development and strong bones.

Essential Nutrients: The consumption of a diverse range of food sources, including meat, fish, and plant-based foods, would have ensured that Neanderthals received many of the essential nutrients they needed to maintain good health. For example, marine resources would have provided omega-3 fatty acids, which are important for brain function and heart health, while plant-based foods would have supplied vitamins, minerals, and dietary fiber.

Energy Balance: The Neanderthal diet was calorie-dense, with a high intake of fat from animal sources. This would have been crucial for maintaining energy balance, especially in the harsh and cold environments they often inhabited.

Negative Impact on Health:

Limited Dietary Diversity: Although Neanderthals consumed a diverse range of foods, their diet was still heavily based on the consumption of large mammals. This reliance on a relatively narrow range of food sources may have made them more vulnerable to fluctuations in the availability of prey, potentially leading to periods of food scarcity and malnutrition.

Pathogens and Parasites: Consuming raw or undercooked meat can expose individuals to various pathogens and parasites. While Neanderthals did use fire for cooking, it is possible that they may have consumed some raw or undercooked meat, potentially leading to illness or parasitic infections.

Dental Health: Neanderthals are known to have experienced dental health issues, such as tooth wear, cavities, and periodontal disease. While the exact causes of these dental problems are not fully understood, it is possible that their diet, which included abrasive foods, such as nuts and seeds, as well as sticky carbohydrates, such as tubers and fruits, may have contributed to dental wear and the development of cavities.

In conclusion, the Neanderthal diet had both positive and negative impacts on their health. While their high protein intake and diverse range of food sources provided essential nutrients and energy, their reliance on a relatively narrow range of food sources and potential exposure to pathogens and parasites may have also had detrimental effects on their health.

Neanderthal-Modern Human Interactions: Encounters and Interbreeding

The First Encounters Between Neanderthals and Modern Humans

The first encounters between Neanderthals and modern humans (Homo sapiens) are a topic of significant interest and debate among researchers, as these interactions had profound implications for both groups. In this section, we will explore the current understanding of when and where these encounters occurred, as well as their potential outcomes and consequences.

When and Where Did the Encounters Occur?

Neanderthals and modern humans are believed to have first encountered each other in Europe and Western Asia between 50,000 and 40,000 years ago. During this time, modern humans were migrating out of Africa and expanding into new territories, while Neanderthals were already well-established in these regions. The exact timing and locations of these encounters are still being studied, but it is clear that there was a period of overlap between the two populations.

What Happened During These Encounters?

There are several possible outcomes and consequences of the first encounters between Neanderthals and modern humans, which include:

Interbreeding: Genetic evidence suggests that there was a limited amount of interbreeding between Neanderthals and modern humans. As a result, non-African human populations today carry a small percentage of Neanderthal DNA. This interbreeding may have occurred during the early encounters between the two groups, and it is possible that these interactions led to the exchange of genes that provided advantageous traits to both populations.

Cultural Exchange: Some researchers believe that the first encounters between Neanderthals and modern humans may have led to the exchange of cultural practices, knowledge, and technology. For example, modern humans may have introduced new stone tool technologies and artistic expressions to Neanderthals, while Neanderthals may have shared their knowledge of local resources and survival strategies.

Competition and Conflict: The arrival of modern humans in Neanderthal territories likely led to competition for resources, such as food, water, and shelter. This competition may have occasionally resulted in conflict between the two groups, as they struggled to secure the resources necessary for their survival.

Disease Transmission: Some researchers have suggested that the arrival of modern humans may have introduced new diseases to Neanderthal populations, to which they had little or no immunity. These diseases could have contributed to the decline and eventual extinction of the Neanderthals.

The Consequences of the Encounters

The first encounters between Neanderthals and modern humans had lasting consequences for both groups. For modern humans, these interactions resulted in the acquisition of a small percentage of Neanderthal DNA, which can still be found in non-African human populations today. For Neanderthals, however, the encounters marked the beginning of their decline, as they faced increased competition for resources, potential conflicts, and possibly the introduction of new diseases. Within a few thousand years of these initial encounters, Neanderthal populations dwindled, and they ultimately became extinct around 40,000 years ago.

In conclusion, the first encounters between Neanderthals and modern humans were complex and multifaceted events that had significant implications for both groups. Through the study of these encounters, researchers can gain valuable insights into the dynamics of human evolution, migration, and the interactions between different hominin species.

Evidence of Interbreeding and Its Implications

Recent advances in genetic research have provided compelling evidence that Neanderthals and modern humans (Homo sapiens) interbred during their time of coexistence. This interbreeding has left a lasting genetic legacy in the form of Neanderthal DNA present in the genomes of modern humans of non-African descent. In this section, we will explore the evidence of interbreeding between Neanderthals and modern humans and discuss the implications of these findings.

Genetic Evidence of Interbreeding:

The most significant evidence of interbreeding between Neanderthals and modern humans comes from the analysis of ancient Neanderthal DNA, as well as the DNA of present-day humans. These genetic studies have revealed that:

- Approximately 1-2% of the DNA of modern humans of non-African descent can be traced back to Neanderthals. This suggests that there was limited interbreeding between the two populations during their time of coexistence.

- The presence of Neanderthal DNA in modern human genomes is not uniformly distributed. Instead, certain regions of the genome have higher levels of Neanderthal ancestry, while other regions have little or no Neanderthal DNA. This pattern suggests that some genes were preferentially retained or lost over time due to natural selection.

Implications of Interbreeding:

The discovery of Neanderthal DNA in modern human genomes has several important implications for our understanding of human evolution, biology, and health:

Adaptive Traits: Some of the Neanderthal genes that have been retained in modern human genomes may have provided advantageous traits that helped our ancestors survive in new and challenging environments. For example, certain Neanderthal genes have been linked to immune system function, suggesting that interbreeding may have bolstered the immune response of modern humans against novel pathogens.

Detrimental Effects: Conversely, some Neanderthal genes may have had negative effects on the health and fitness of modern humans. For instance, certain Neanderthal gene variants have been associated with an increased risk of developing conditions such as type 2 diabetes, lupus, and Crohn's disease.

Human Evolution and Migration: The presence of Neanderthal DNA in modern human genomes provides further evidence that our ancestors migrated out of Africa and encountered Neanderthals in Europe and Asia. This genetic legacy also suggests that the interactions between the two populations were not solely antagonistic but also involved some degree of cooperation and integration.

Cultural Exchange: The evidence of interbreeding between Neanderthals and modern humans raises the possibility that there may have been cultural exchanges between the two groups. This could have included the sharing of knowledge, tools, and techniques that contributed to the survival and success of both populations.

In conclusion, the evidence of interbreeding between Neanderthals and modern humans has shed new light on the complex relationships between these two hominin species. The genetic legacy of Neanderthals within modern human genomes provides insights into the adaptive and detrimental effects of these ancient gene variants, as well as the broader implications for our understanding of human evolution, migration, and cultural exchange.

Genetic Legacy: Neanderthal DNA in Modern Humans

The discovery of Neanderthal DNA in the genomes of modern humans has generated considerable interest and excitement in the fields of genetics, anthropology, and human evolution. This genetic legacy, which can be traced back to the interbreeding between Neanderthals and modern humans during their time of coexistence, has important implications for our understanding of human history and biology. In this section, we will delve into the presence and impact of Neanderthal DNA in modern humans.

Distribution of Neanderthal DNA in Modern Humans:

The presence of Neanderthal DNA in modern human genomes is not uniform across all populations. Studies have shown that:

Humans of non-African descent carry about 1-2% Neanderthal DNA in their genome, while humans of African descent have little (about 0.3%) or no Neanderthal ancestry. This pattern reflects the fact that interbreeding between Neanderthals and modern humans occurred primarily after the latter migrated out of Africa and encountered Neanderthals in Europe and Asia.

The distribution of Neanderthal DNA within individual genomes is also not uniform. Some genomic regions have a higher proportion of Neanderthal ancestry, while others have little or none. This pattern suggests that certain Neanderthal gene variants were selectively retained or lost over time, likely due to the effects of natural selection.

Impact of Neanderthal DNA on Modern Human Biology and Health:

The presence of Neanderthal DNA in modern human genomes has both positive and negative implications for human biology and health:

Adaptive Traits: Some Neanderthal gene variants are thought to have conferred advantageous traits to modern humans, helping them adapt to new environments and challenges. Examples of such traits include improved immune system function, which may have protected modern humans against novel pathogens, and adaptations related to skin and hair characteristics, which could have helped them better cope with varying climate conditions.

Detrimental Effects: On the other hand, some Neanderthal gene variants have been associated with negative health effects in modern humans. For instance, certain Neanderthal gene variants have been linked to an increased risk of developing conditions such as type 2 diabetes, lupus, Crohn's disease, and even depression.

Understanding Human Evolution: The presence of Neanderthal DNA in modern human genomes offers valuable insights into the complex history of human evolution and migration. It highlights the fact that the interactions between Neanderthals and modern humans were not solely competitive but also involved a degree of cooperation, integration, and gene flow between the two populations.

In summary, the genetic legacy of Neanderthals in modern humans provides a fascinating window into the past, revealing the intricate relationships between these two hominin species. The presence of Neanderthal DNA in modern human genomes has both adaptive and detrimental effects on human biology and health, and it offers important insights into the broader context of human evolution, migration, and cultural exchange.

The Mysterious Disappearance: Extinction of the Neanderthals

Theories Explaining the Neanderthal Extinction

The extinction of Neanderthals around 40,000 years ago remains one of the most intriguing mysteries in the field of human evolution. Over the years, various theories have been proposed to explain the disappearance of this hominin species, ranging from competition with modern humans to climate change. In this section, we will explore some of the most prominent theories explaining the Neanderthal extinction.

Competition with Modern Humans: One leading theory suggests that the arrival of modern humans (Homo sapiens) in Europe and Asia led to competition for resources such as food, water, and shelter. This competition may have put pressure on Neanderthal populations, ultimately leading to their decline and extinction. Modern humans may have had advantages in technology, social organization, and innovation, which could have helped them outcompete Neanderthals for the same resources.

Climate Change: Another theory posits that rapid and severe climate fluctuations during the time of Neanderthal extinction played a significant role in their demise. Neanderthals were well-adapted to cold environments, but the sudden and dramatic shifts in temperature and environmental conditions may have disrupted their food sources and habitats, making it difficult for them to adapt and survive.

Disease Transmission: Some researchers propose that the arrival of modern humans may have introduced new diseases to Neanderthal populations, to which they had little or no immunity. These diseases could have spread rapidly through Neanderthal communities, leading to population decline and eventual extinction.

Interbreeding with Modern Humans: Another theory suggests that interbreeding between Neanderthals and modern humans played a role in the Neanderthal extinction. While limited gene flow occurred between the two populations, it is possible that this interbreeding contributed to the dilution and eventual disappearance of the Neanderthal gene pool, as Neanderthal genes became absorbed into the modern human population.

Small Population Size and Reduced Genetic Diversity: Neanderthals are believed to have had relatively small population sizes and reduced genetic diversity compared to modern humans. This lack of genetic diversity may have made them more vulnerable to environmental changes, disease, and other pressures, leading to their decline and eventual extinction.

It is important to note that the Neanderthal extinction was likely a complex process involving multiple factors, rather than being driven solely by one cause. A combination of competition with modern humans, climate change, disease transmission, interbreeding, and reduced genetic diversity may have all played a part in the disappearance of this fascinating hominin species.

In conclusion, the extinction of Neanderthals remains an ongoing area of research, with new discoveries and insights constantly emerging. Understanding the factors that led to their extinction not only sheds light on the complex history of human evolution but also provides valuable lessons about the challenges and vulnerabilities faced by species in the face of environmental change and competition.

Environmental Factors and Climate Change

Environmental factors and climate change have played a crucial role in shaping the evolution, adaptation, and survival of species throughout Earth's history. These factors have influenced ecosystems, habitats, and the distribution and abundance of resources, creating challenges and opportunities for various species, including humans and their ancestors. In this section, we will discuss the impacts of environmental factors and climate change on human evolution, with a focus on Neanderthals and modern humans.

Impact on Neanderthals:

Adaptation to Cold Climates: Neanderthals were well-adapted to the cold climates of Europe and Western Asia during the Ice Age. Their stocky body build, shorter limbs, and other physical features were advantageous in conserving heat and surviving in harsh, cold environments.

Food Resources: Neanderthals had to adapt their hunting strategies, diet, and food processing techniques to the changing environment. As the climate shifted, so did the availability of plant and animal resources. Neanderthals relied heavily on large game animals, such as mammoths and reindeer, which may have become less abundant due to climate change and habitat loss.

Possible Role in Extinction: As previously mentioned, climate change has been proposed as one of the factors contributing to the Neanderthal extinction. Rapid and severe climate fluctuations may have disrupted Neanderthal food sources and habitats, making it difficult for them to adapt and survive.

Impact on Modern Humans:

Migration and Dispersal: Climate change has been a significant driver of human migration and dispersal throughout history. For example, changing environmental conditions and the availability of resources likely played a role in the migration of modern humans out of Africa and their subsequent spread across Europe, Asia, and other parts of the world.

Adaptive Traits and Technology: The need to adapt to changing environments and climates spurred the development of new technologies, social structures, and cultural practices in modern humans. This includes the development of more sophisticated tools, clothing, and shelter, as well as innovations in food processing and storage techniques.

Impact on Health and Disease: Changing environmental conditions can also have implications for human health and disease. For instance, climate change can influence the distribution and prevalence of infectious diseases, as well as the availability and quality of food resources, which in turn can affect human health and well-being.

In conclusion, environmental factors and climate change have had a profound impact on human evolution and the development of both Neanderthals and modern humans. These factors have shaped the ways in which our ancestors adapted to their environments, developed new technologies and strategies for survival, and ultimately influenced the course of human history. As climate change continues to be a pressing issue today, understanding the impacts of environmental factors on human evolution can provide valuable insights into our own vulnerability and resilience in the face of a changing world.

Competition and Possible Conflicts with Modern Humans

The arrival of modern humans (Homo sapiens) in Europe and Asia around 45,000 years ago led to a period of overlap and interaction with Neanderthals, who had already been inhabiting these regions for hundreds of thousands of years. This coexistence likely involved competition for resources and possibly conflicts between the two hominin species. In this section, we will explore the nature of the competition and potential conflicts between Neanderthals and modern humans.

Competition for Resources:

Food: Both Neanderthals and modern humans relied on hunting and gathering for sustenance. They may have competed for the same game animals and plant resources, particularly in regions where these resources were scarce or seasonal. Modern humans may have had advantages in hunting techniques, tool technology, and cooperative strategies, which could have given them an edge in securing food resources.

Shelter: Access to suitable shelter was essential for survival during the harsh climatic conditions of the Ice Age. Neanderthals and modern humans may have competed for prime locations that offered protection from the elements, access to fresh water, and proximity to food resources.

Territory: The establishment and defense of territories were likely essential for both Neanderthal and modern human groups. Competition for territory could have led to conflicts and confrontations between these hominin species, particularly in regions where suitable habitats were limited.

Possible Conflicts:

Direct Confrontations: While there is limited direct evidence of violent encounters between Neanderthals and modern humans, it is possible that conflicts arose due to competition for resources or territorial disputes. Instances of interpersonal violence have been observed in both Neanderthal and modern human fossil remains, suggesting that aggression and conflict were not uncommon in the prehistoric world.

Indirect Pressure: Modern humans may have exerted indirect pressure on Neanderthal populations by outcompeting them for resources or displacing them from their preferred habitats. This pressure could have led to a decline in Neanderthal population size, making them more vulnerable to other factors such as climate change and disease.

Cultural Differences: Differences in social organization, technology, and cultural practices may have contributed to competition and potential conflicts between Neanderthals and modern humans. For example, modern humans may have had more complex social structures and communication systems, which could have facilitated better cooperation and resource sharing within their groups, giving them a competitive advantage over Neanderthals.

It is important to note that interactions between Neanderthals and modern humans were likely complex and varied, involving not only competition and potential conflicts but also cooperation, cultural exchange, and interbreeding. Understanding the nature of these interactions can provide valuable insights into the factors that contributed to the eventual extinction of Neanderthals and the success of modern humans in colonizing diverse environments and overcoming various challenges.

Unearthing the Past: Neanderthal Fossils and Archaeological Discoveries

Notable Neanderthal Fossil Finds

The study of Neanderthal fossils has been integral to our understanding of this hominin species and its place in human evolution. Over the years, numerous Neanderthal fossil finds have provided valuable insights into their physical characteristics, behavior, and cultural practices. In this section, we will discuss some of the most notable Neanderthal fossil finds and their significance.

Feldhofer Cave, Germany (1856): The first Neanderthal fossil discovery was made in the Feldhofer Cave in the Neander Valley, Germany, in 1856. This find consisted of a skullcap, several limb bones, and a pelvis, which were initially believed to belong to a modern human with pathological deformities. The discovery later led to the recognition of Neanderthals as a distinct hominin species and marked the beginning of Neanderthal research.

La Chapelle-aux-Saints, France (1908): The discovery of a nearly complete Neanderthal skeleton in La Chapelle-aux-Saints, France, provided crucial insights into Neanderthal anatomy and posture. The skeleton, known as the „Old Man of La Chapelle," revealed that Neanderthals had a stocky build, a large braincase, and other features distinct from modern humans. This find also provided evidence of intentional burial, suggesting that Neanderthals may have had complex cultural practices and beliefs.

Shanidar Cave, Iraq (1950s-1960s): The discovery of multiple Neanderthal skeletons in the Shanidar Cave in Iraq provided important information about Neanderthal social structure, care for the injured, and burial practices. One individual, known as Shanidar 1, showed evidence of multiple injuries and disabilities, suggesting that Neanderthal groups took care of their injured and disabled members. The presence of pollen in the burial site of another individual, Shanidar 4, has been interpreted by some as evidence of a „flower burial," indicating a possible ritualistic element to Neanderthal burial practices.

Kebara Cave, Israel (1982): The discovery of a well-preserved Neanderthal skeleton, known as Kebara 2 or „Moshe," in the Kebara Cave in Israel provided valuable information about Neanderthal anatomy, particularly the ribcage and spine. This find also included a well-preserved hyoid bone, which is important for understanding the possible vocal abilities and language capabilities of Neanderthals.

Sima de los Huesos, Spain (1990s-present): The Sima de los Huesos („Pit of Bones") site in Spain has yielded an extraordinary collection of hominin fossils, including numerous Neanderthal remains. This site has provided insights into the early stages of Neanderthal evolution, as well as evidence of interpersonal violence and possible cannibalism.

Denisova Cave, Siberia (2008): Although not a Neanderthal fossil find, the discovery of a finger bone belonging to a previously unknown hominin species, the Denisovans, in the Denisova Cave in Siberia has important implications for our understanding of Neanderthal evolution and interactions. Genetic analysis has revealed that Neanderthals, Denisovans, and modern humans share a common ancestry and interbred with one another during their time of coexistence.

These notable Neanderthal fossil finds have significantly advanced our understanding of this fascinating hominin species, shedding light on their anatomy, behavior, and culture. Ongoing research and new discoveries continue to enrich our knowledge of Neanderthals and their place in human evolution.

The Role of Archaeology in Understanding Neanderthal Life

Archaeology plays a crucial role in our understanding of Neanderthal life, as it allows us to piece together evidence from the past and reconstruct the day-to-day existence of these hominins. Through the examination of artifacts, fossils, and other material remains, archaeologists can gain insights into the physical, behavioral, and cultural aspects of Neanderthal life. In this section, we will discuss the role of archaeology in expanding our understanding of Neanderthal life.

Physical Evidence:

Fossil Remains: The study of Neanderthal fossil remains provides important information about their anatomy, physiology, and health. By examining skeletal features and comparing them with those of other hominins and modern humans, archaeologists can gain insights into the unique adaptations and evolutionary history of Neanderthals.

Isotopic Analysis: By analyzing stable isotopes in Neanderthal bones and teeth, archaeologists can reconstruct aspects of their diet, such as the types of plants and animals they consumed and their reliance on different food sources.

Behavioral Evidence:

Stone Tools: The study of Neanderthal stone tool technology, particularly the Mousterian industry, provides insights into their cognitive abilities, problem-solving skills, and resource exploitation strategies. By examining the types of tools they created, the raw materials they used, and the methods of tool production, archaeologists can better understand the behavioral patterns and technological innovations of Neanderthals.

Site Formation Processes: The analysis of Neanderthal archaeological sites and their formation processes can provide valuable information about the organization of their living spaces, their use of resources, and their interaction with the environment. This includes understanding the spatial distribution of artifacts and features within a site, as well as the processes that led to their deposition and preservation.

Cultural Evidence:

Art and Symbolic Expression: The discovery of potential Neanderthal art and symbolic expressions, such as engraved objects, pigment use, and personal ornaments, has prompted archaeologists to reevaluate the cognitive and cultural capabilities of these hominins. Such finds suggest that Neanderthals may have had more advanced cognitive abilities and complex cultural practices than previously assumed.

Burial Practices: The study of Neanderthal burial practices and associated grave goods provides insights into their beliefs about death and the afterlife, as well as their social structure and group dynamics. The presence of intentional burials and possible ritualistic elements suggests that Neanderthals may have had complex cultural practices and beliefs similar to those of modern humans.

By combining the evidence obtained through archaeological research with other lines of inquiry, such as paleoanthropology, genetics, and paleoclimatology, we can build a more comprehensive understanding of Neanderthal life. This interdisciplinary approach allows us to explore the full range of Neanderthal experiences, from their physical adaptations to their behavioral patterns and cultural practices, and to better understand their place in human evolution.

Modern Techniques for Analyzing Neanderthal Remains

Advancements in scientific techniques and technology have revolutionized the study of Neanderthal remains, allowing researchers to gain new insights into this hominin species' biology, behavior, and culture. In this section, we will discuss some of the modern techniques used for analyzing Neanderthal remains and the information they can provide.

Genetic Analysis: The advent of ancient DNA (aDNA) analysis has significantly advanced our understanding of Neanderthal evolution, population dynamics, and interactions with other hominins. By extracting and sequencing DNA from Neanderthal fossils, researchers can study genetic relationships between Neanderthal populations, as well as their relationships with modern humans and other hominin species like Denisovans.

Isotopic Analysis: Stable isotope analysis of Neanderthal bones and teeth can provide valuable information about their diet and ecology. By analyzing the ratios of different isotopes (e.g., carbon, nitrogen, and oxygen), researchers can reconstruct aspects of Neanderthal diet, such as the types of plants and animals they consumed, their reliance on different food sources, and their movement patterns.

Microscopic Wear Analysis: By examining microscopic wear patterns on Neanderthal teeth, researchers can gain insights into their diet and food processing techniques. Dental microwear analysis can reveal information about the types of foods consumed, the texture of those foods, and the methods used for food preparation, such as cooking or grinding.

Computed Tomography (CT) Scanning: CT scanning allows for the non-destructive examination of Neanderthal fossils, providing detailed information about their internal structures. This technique can be used to study the internal anatomy of Neanderthal bones and teeth, as well as to reconstruct their brain morphology and infer aspects of their cognitive abilities.

Microscopic Analysis of Stone Tools: The use of microscopy to study Neanderthal stone tools can reveal important details about their production techniques, use-wear, and the types of activities they were involved in. By examining microscopic wear patterns on stone tools, researchers can infer the materials they were used to process (e.g., wood, hide, or meat) and the techniques employed in their use.

Spatial Analysis and Geographic Information Systems (GIS): The use of spatial analysis and GIS tools allows researchers to study the distribution of Neanderthal artifacts and features within archaeological sites, as well as their broader landscape context. This can provide insights into the organization of their living spaces, their mobility patterns, and their interaction with the environment.

Proteomic Analysis: The study of ancient proteins preserved in Neanderthal remains can provide information about their diet, health, and even aspects of their social behavior. By identifying and analyzing the types of proteins preserved in Neanderthal fossils, researchers can gain insights into their dietary preferences, exposure to pathogens, and possible social inter-actions.

These modern techniques have greatly enhanced our ability to analyze Neanderthal remains and uncover new information about their biology, behavior, and culture. As technology continues to advance, we can expect further breakthroughs in our understanding of this fascinating hominin species and its place in human evolution.

Advancements in Neanderthal Research: Decoding the Neanderthal Genome

The Neanderthal Genome Project

The Neanderthal Genome Project is an international scientific endeavor aimed at sequencing and analyzing the complete Neanderthal genome. This groundbreaking research has revolutionized our understanding of Neanderthal biology, evolution, and interactions with other hominins, including modern humans. In this section, we will discuss the objectives, methods, and major findings of the Neanderthal Genome Project.

Objectives:

- The primary goal of the Neanderthal Genome Project is to obtain a comprehensive understanding of the genetic makeup of Neanderthals. This knowledge can help researchers to:
- Investigate the evolutionary history of Neanderthals and their relationship with other hominins.
- Identify the genetic differences and similarities between Neanderthals and modern humans.
- Explore the potential consequences of interbreeding between Neanderthals and modern humans.
- Determine the genetic factors underlying Neanderthal adaptations to their environment and unique physical traits.

Methods:

- The Neanderthal Genome Project relies on the extraction, sequencing, and analysis of ancient DNA (aDNA) from Neanderthal fossils. The process involves:
- Obtaining well-preserved Neanderthal fossil samples, such as bones or teeth.
- Extracting aDNA from these samples using specialized laboratory techniques.
- Sequencing the extracted DNA using high-throughput sequencing technologies.
- Analyzing and comparing the sequenced Neanderthal genome with the genomes of modern humans and other hominins to identify genetic differences and similarities.

Major Findings:

- The Neanderthal Genome Project has led to several significant discoveries, which have reshaped our understanding of Neanderthal biology and evolution. Some key findings include:
- Neanderthal-Modern Human Interbreeding: The Neanderthal genome analysis revealed that Neanderthals and modern humans interbred, with approximately 1-2% of the DNA of non-African modern humans being of Neanderthal origin. This finding indicates that gene flow occurred between the two species, suggesting a more complex interaction history than previously assumed.

Adaptive Introgression: The analysis of Neanderthal DNA in modern humans has identified several gene variants that were likely beneficial to our ancestors and have been passed on through generations. These genes are associated with various traits, such as immune system function, skin and hair pigmentation, and metabolic processes.

Cognitive and Developmental Differences: Comparisons of the Neanderthal and modern human genomes have identified genetic differences related to cognitive development and brain function. While the exact implications of these differences remain uncertain, they may have contributed to the distinct cognitive abilities and behaviors of Neanderthals.

Population Dynamics: The Neanderthal Genome Project has provided insights into the population dynamics and genetic diversity of Neanderthals. Studies have revealed that Neanderthal populations were relatively small and isolated, which may have contributed to their eventual extinction.

The Neanderthal Genome Project has significantly advanced our understanding of this hominin species and its place in human evolution. As research continues and new techniques emerge, we can expect to learn even more about the genetic legacy and fascinating history of Neanderthals.

Insights Gained from Genetic Research

Genetic research has revolutionized our understanding of human biology, evolution, and history. By studying DNA and the genetic information it encodes, scientists have made significant discoveries that shed light on various aspects of human life, from our ancestry to our susceptibility to diseases. In this section, we will discuss some of the key insights gained from genetic research.

Human Evolution and Migration: Genetic research has helped us to trace the origins of modern humans and map our migration patterns across the globe. By comparing genetic variations among different human populations, scientists have been able to reconstruct our evolutionary history, pinpointing our origins in Africa and revealing the subsequent migrations that led to the global distribution of human populations.

Ancestry and Genealogy: Advances in genetic testing have made it possible for individuals to explore their personal ancestry and genealogy. DNA tests can reveal information about a person's ethnic background, migration patterns of their ancestors, and even connections to specific historical figures or events.

Interbreeding between Hominin Species: Genetic research has revealed that modern humans interbred with other hominin species, such as Neanderthals and Denisovans. This has led to the discovery that a small percentage of the DNA of non-African modern humans is of Neanderthal or Denisovan origin, providing insights into the complex interactions between these species in our evolutionary past.

Genetic Basis of Disease: By identifying the genes and genetic mutations associated with specific diseases, researchers have been able to gain a better understanding of the underlying biological mechanisms and develop more targeted treatments. Genetic research has also led to the development of personalized medicine, where treatments can be tailored to an individual's genetic profile.

Genetic Adaptation: Genetic research has shed light on how human populations have adapted to different environments and challenges over time. For example, studies have identified specific genetic adaptations related to altitude tolerance, resistance to infectious diseases, and dietary preferences, among others.

Epigenetics: The study of epigenetics has revealed that environmental factors can influence gene expression and that these changes can be passed on to future generations. This research has significant implications for understanding the complex interplay between genes and the environment in human health and development.

Gene Editing Technologies: Advances in genetic research have led to the development of powerful gene editing tools, such as CRISPR-Cas9, which have the potential to revolutionize medicine, agriculture, and other fields. These technologies enable precise manipulation of DNA sequences, allowing for the correction of genetic mutations or the introduction of new genetic traits.

In conclusion, genetic research has provided invaluable insights into various aspects of human biology, evolution, and history. As our understanding of the human genome continues to grow, we can expect even more groundbreaking discoveries and applications that will help to shape our future.

Ethical Considerations in Neanderthal Research

Neanderthal research, like any scientific field, is accompanied by ethical considerations that must be taken into account to ensure responsible and respectful conduct. As we explore the biology, behavior, and culture of this extinct hominin species, researchers must navigate the complex ethical landscape surrounding the study of ancient human relatives. In this section, we will discuss some of the key ethical considerations in Neanderthal research.

Treatment of Human Remains: Neanderthal fossils are the remains of once-living individuals who had their own unique experiences, relationships, and identities. As such, researchers must handle these remains with respect and dignity. This includes proper storage, conservation, and display of the fossils, as well as ensuring that they are not used in ways that may be seen as disrespectful or exploitative.

Indigenous Rights and Cultural Sensitivity: Neanderthal remains and artifacts are often found in areas that have been inhabited by indigenous peoples for thousands of years. Researchers must be sensitive to the cultural and historical connections that these communities may have to the remains and work collaboratively with them in the research process. This can involve obtaining permission to study the remains, sharing findings with the community, and respecting any cultural practices or beliefs surrounding the remains.

Scientific Integrity and Transparency: Neanderthal research, like any scientific field, must be guided by principles of scientific integrity and transparency. Researchers must be honest in their reporting of findings, avoid exaggerating or misrepresenting the significance of their work, and be open to critique and revision as new evidence comes to light. Additionally, researchers should strive to make their data and methods publicly available to promote reproducibility and collaboration within the scientific community.

Biological and Genetic Research: The study of Neanderthal genetics raises unique ethical considerations, particularly with regard to potential applications in biotechnology and medicine. For example, the idea of using gene editing technologies to recreate Neanderthals or introduce Neanderthal genes into modern humans raises questions about the ethical boundaries of genetic manipulation and the potential consequences of such actions.

Intellectual Property and Commercialization: As Neanderthal research often involves the discovery of new knowledge and technologies, researchers must consider the ethical implications of intellectual property and commercialization. This includes ensuring that the benefits of research are shared equitably, both within the scientific community and with the broader public, and avoiding the commodification or exploitation of Neanderthal remains or knowledge for financial gain.

Public Communication and Education: Neanderthal research has the potential to captivate public interest and inform our understanding of human evolution. Researchers have a responsibility to communicate their findings accurately and responsibly, avoiding sensationalism and misrepresentation that may perpetuate myths or misconceptions about Neanderthals. They should also strive to promote public education and engagement with the scientific process.

In conclusion, Neanderthal research, like any scientific field, must navigate a complex ethical landscape to ensure that the pursuit of knowledge is conducted responsibly and respectfully. By acknowledging and addressing these ethical considerations, researchers can contribute to a better understanding of our ancient human relatives while maintaining the highest standards of scientific integrity and respect for human dignity.

Conclusion: The Enduring Legacy of Neanderthals

Throughout this book, we have embarked on a captivating journey to uncover the mysteries surrounding Neanderthals, their evolutionary history, physical characteristics, culture, technological advancements, and interactions with modern humans. As we continue to unravel the secrets of our ancient relatives, it is important to recognize the significance of studying Neanderthals. They offer not only invaluable insights into our own evolutionary history but also serve as a testament to the remarkable adaptability and resilience of the human species. By understanding the lives of Neanderthals, we can gain a deeper appreciation of our place in the world and our shared human narrative.

Neanderthal research has transformed our understanding of human evolution and the complex interplay between biology, environment, and culture. As we continue to make new discoveries, we must also grapple with the ethical considerations surrounding the study of ancient human remains, ensuring that our pursuit of knowledge is respectful and responsible.

The legacy of Neanderthals lives on in the DNA of modern humans, a testament to the intricate web of connections that binds us to our ancient ancestors. As we look to the future, it is our responsibility to honor and preserve the memory of Neanderthals, using the lessons we have learned from their lives to better understand ourselves and our place in the natural world.

Other books by the author

The author:
Heinz G. Saenger
Lives since 2020 with his
second wife in Thailand

"Feng Shui: Background, Meaning, Application and Social Added Value" is a comprehensive guide to the fascinating world of Feng Shui. This book offers a deep insight into the history and origin of Feng Shui, the connection to Taoism and the meaning of the five elements. It also presents practical applications of Feng Shui in architecture, design and daily life. Discover how creating harmony and balance in your environment can enhance your well-being and make a positive contribution to society and the environment.

Feng Shui

Heinz G. Saenger

KRATOM FOR NEWBIES

All You Need To Know About Kratom Usage

By *Heinz Guenther Saenger*

NEANDERTHALS

Made in the USA
Coppell, TX
15 May 2024

32435322R00059